Malorie The Mindful Moment

MANAGING BIG EMOTIONS WITH MINDFULNESS

Written By
Kaci Sage

Illustrated By
Vlada Zinchenko

Copyright © 2021 by Indigo Coyote Publications

All rights reserved. No part of this publication or the information in it may be quoted or reproduced in any form or by any means, electronic or mechanical, including photocopying, recording, or by any information storage and retrieval system, without prior written permission of the copyright holder.

ISBN 978-1-957247-01-4

eISBN 978-1-957247-00-7

For my sweet little Arbor Moon:

Thank you for choosing me to be your mama. May you always remember that you're made of magic and hold everything you could ever need right inside.

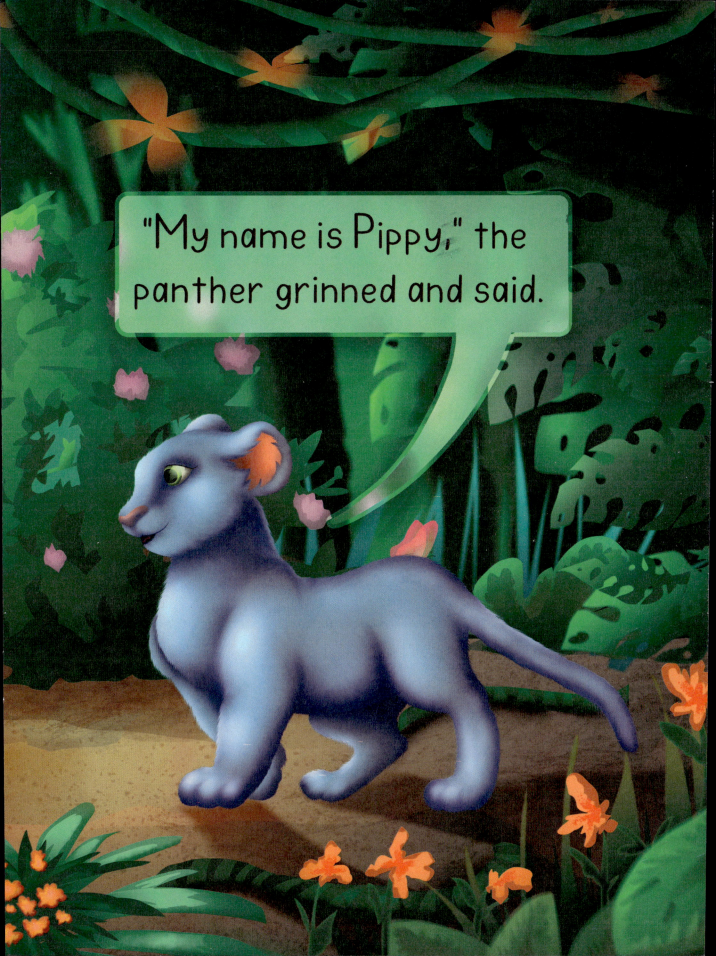
"My name is Pippy," the panther grinned and said.

Malorie the monkey swung from vine to vine;
She bounced from branch to branch, having the best time!

She couldn't see her new friend way up there in the trees, But she *knew* she'd be faster than earth-bound Pippy!

Malorie giggled happily as the wind kissed her face. "There it is! I see the waterfall!" She'd soon win the race.

Then Malorie plopped down from the trees to the gushing waterfall.

"I did it! I won!"

She cheered proudly, feeling 20 feet tall!

Malorie picked a ripe yellow banana off a nearby tree; And she munched away while waiting for Pippy.

SURPRISE! Out from the bushes popped her hiding pal Pippy!

Malorie couldn't believe it, and she shouted out loud: "Have you been here all this time?!"

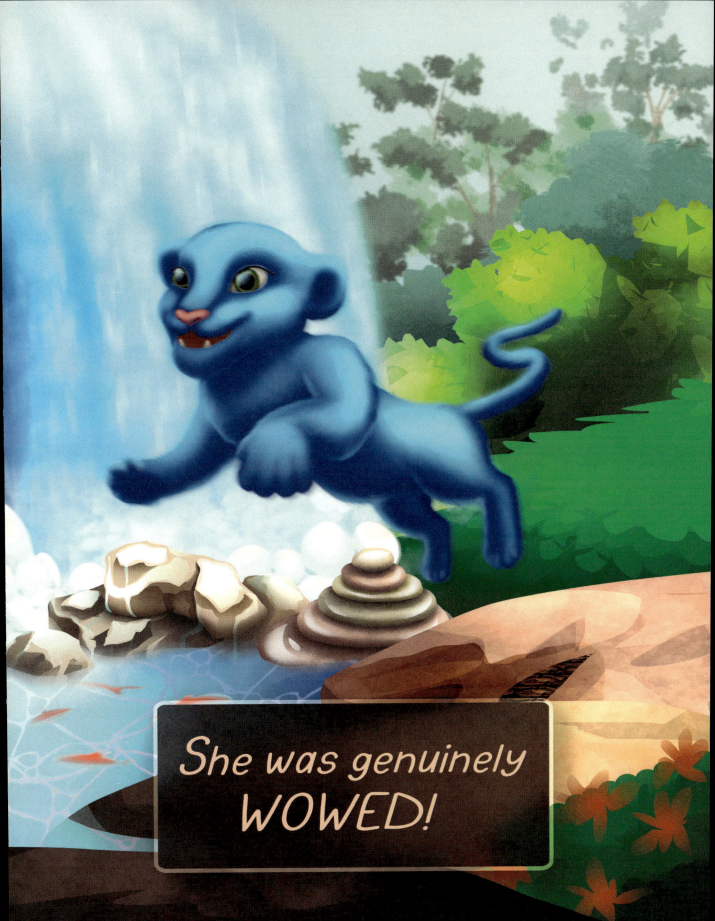

But Malorie remembered something her mama taught her; A tool she could use when she got angry or bothered.

Mindful Malorie breathed in deep and felt into her heart. She was a bit overwhelmed and didn't know where to start.

But she just kept breathing until she started to feel calm. She concentrated hard and thought of her sweet mom.

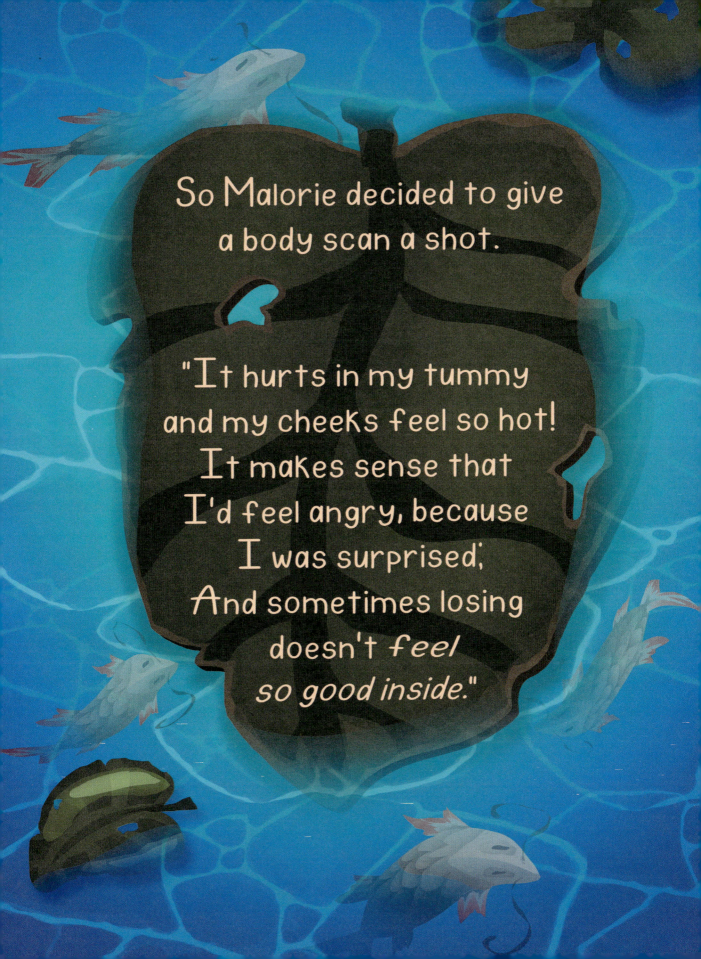

So Malorie decided to give a body scan a shot.

"It hurts in my tummy and my cheeks feel so hot! It makes sense that I'd feel angry, because I was surprised; And sometimes losing doesn't *feel* so good inside."

With an exhale, she imagined her anger floating up to the sky. She felt calmer and peaceful, and so light she could fly!

Malorie felt great relief by allowing her heart to steer. Her mom's mindful tips helped quiet her mind without fear.

"Breathing deep in my chest and feeling love in my heart, I repeat happy thoughts, 'I am safe, strong, and smart!'

It may not all go away super fast, But it helps me to realize these feelings won't last!"

Malorie felt so much better, got up, and turned around. She praised, "good job, Pippy! You're so fast on the ground!"

She smiled and told her friend that she was proud, Then released her tough feelings up to the clouds.

All in all, Malorie was really proud of herself, too. She had a tough situation and remembered what to do.

And the next time she feels a big emotion, she knows she can sit down, close her eyes, and inside she can go!

ABOUT THE AUTHOR:

Kaci Sage is a passionate writer and guided meditation teacher specializing in self-awareness, emotional development, and earth-based connection. As a new mom, she's excited to create engaging ways to develop mindfulness and strong emotional processing habits early on in our precious future generations. Doing so fosters happier, healthier lives and a kinder world.

She lives with her family in Northwest Montana where she enjoys cooking, singing and dancing, and hiking in the abundant natural beauty that surrounds her.

Find her latest book releases, listen to guided meditations, or explore her other unique offerings by visiting kacisage.com

ABOUT THE ILLUSTRATOR:

Vlada was blessed to be born into a creative family. Even as a child, Vlada began to portray the beauty she experienced in the world through numerous different creative mediums. As a teenager, she learned that you can be anything you choose in life. Yes, even a tattoo artist. And so, she did!

Passionate about sharing her perspectives and conveying messages for adults through her visuals, she became fascinated by the idea of how to show the beauty of the world to children. She finds the transition from black tattoos to brightly colored book illustrations thrilling and invigorating.

Vlada lives in Ukraine and firmly believes that "love is creativity, and creativity is love." She's excited to expand her work in this field and bring joy to the children of the world through her art.

See her work at vladyzz.artstation.com or contact vz2821@gmail.com for professional inquiries.

Bonus Gift!
Affirmation Coloring Cards

Bring Malorie & Pippy to life with color, cut on the hearts, and practice mindfulness by reading these postive affirmations every day!

I am safe

I am strong

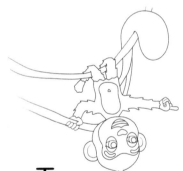

I am smart

I am worthy

I am kind

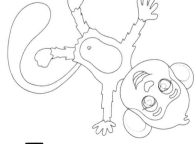

I am capable

Made in the USA
Middletown, DE
05 December 2021